Original title:
Petals in the Rain

Copyright © 2025 Creative Arts Management OÜ
All rights reserved.

Author: Victor Mercer
ISBN HARDBACK: 978-1-80581-888-5
ISBN PAPERBACK: 978-1-80581-415-3
ISBN EBOOK: 978-1-80581-888-5

Raindrops on Silk Flowers

A droplet slips, just like a cat,
It missed the leaf, and lands right flat.
The blooms all giggle, arms out wide,
As puddles start their playful slide.

When skies get grumpy, flowers prance,
They twirl in water, take a chance,
With colors gleaming, jolts of fun,
They splash and laugh, till day is done.

Fragile Colors in the Storm

A purple daisy wears a grin,
As storm clouds gather, it jumps in.
The blues are swirling, what a show!
While raindrops dance, we laugh and glow.

The tulips tiptoe, dodging drops,
With bouncy moves, they twist and flop.
In every storm, a joke we find,
As nature smiles, we leave care behind.

Nature's Tears on Blossom

The daisies bask in a soggy flood,
They giggle at the muddy thud.
One plucky rose, it leaps with glee,
Sailing on waves, wild and free.

A drip rolls down, a soft parade,
While laughing blooms start the charade.
They throw a party in the mud,
And waltz away from nature's flood.

Harmony in Wet Splendor

The wind's a joker, sways the trees,
While laughing blooms say, "Oh, please!"
They play hopscotch, splashing wide,
In a slippery dance, they take pride.

With colors dancing, bright and bold,
Together they break the damp and cold.
Each raindrop sings, a comical tune,
As flowers chuckle beneath the moon.

Drenched Emotions of the Earth

Little droplets dance and sway,
On flowers having their own play.
They giggle as they slip and slide,
While roots beneath just smile with pride.

Mud pies fly, a squishy delight,
As worms join in the soggy fight.
Beeches bow, get a peep show,
A comedy show in nature's flow.

Veils of Flora in the Mist

Fluffy clouds tease shy blooms bright,
Winking at them with morning light.
The daffodils catch a cheeky breeze,
Strutting like stars, they do as they please.

Pansies bloom with a wink and smile,
Making the ground look extra wile.
Chasing the raindrops, giggles entwine,
A festival of giggles, oh, how divine!

Reverie for the Disturbed Garden

Whispers echo through the leafy shade,
As squirrels plot a silly parade.
Chasing tails and teasing each other,
They cause quite the ruckus, oh brother!

Rabbits chuckle as they prance,
In puddles, they take a wild chance.
Jumping high with splashes galore,
It's a raucous mess we can't ignore!

A Liquid Canvas of Bloom

Dripping colors on the soft green,
Nature's humor is felt and seen.
A brush with tulips, staying afloat,
As daisies decide to fashion a coat.

Floral laughter fills the air,
Each blossom a quirky millionaire.
Making the splatters their canvas blue,
A drippy art show, just for you!

Reverie of Blooming Shadows

Beneath the clouds with silly grins,
A dance of colors as laughter spins.
Flowers giggle with a splash and shake,
While worms in slick suits choose to partake.

Sunbeams peek through a misty veil,
Watching the raindrops as they derail.
A turtle in boots slides off for fun,
Sipping puddles 'til the day is done.

Caress of the Chromatic Rain

The squirrels wear hats made of every hue,
Dashing around like they haven't a clue.
The raindrops bounce on rooftop drums,
As ants in tuxedos march to their chums.

With each splash, a tickle and giggle,
The flowers erupt in a cheerful wiggle.
"Who needs umbrellas?" they cheer with glee,
"We're dressed to the nines, come dance with me!"

Rain-kissed Whispers of Life

In puddles deep, reflections lie,
A rabbit jumps high to reach the sky.
His floppy ears droop in watery pools,
Making mud pies, breaking all the rules.

The daisies squeal as drops tap dance,
Their petals slurping up every chance.
Corny jokes drift on the breeze,
While ladybugs wear tiny spritzed parise.

A Tapestry of Tears and Tints

A rainbow slides down the slippery lane,
Bouncing about like a lost refrain.
Giggly glances from the bees in suits,
Buzzing softly, pulling on their roots.

The road gets painted with splashes so bold,
Like a crayon box that did not fold.
Grab your galoshes, let's skip on the glow,
Who knew blue puddles could steal the show?

Shades of Softness and Storm

Fluffy clouds in a tussle,
Drizzles make flowers giggle,
Soft colors splatter the ground,
Wobbly bees dance all around.

When the thunder starts to grumble,
Blossoms sway as if to stumble,
Little bugs don their raincoats,
Hopping like they've lost their boats.

A squirrel spins in the puddles,
While a cat just shakes and cuddles,
With a splash and a joyful pounce,
All the blooms begin to bounce.

Harlequin hues burst through gloom,
In the park, they start to zoom,
Laughter drips from every leaf,
As clouds laugh at their own mischief.

Fragments of Beauty in Motion

Raindrops race in a wild spree,
Chasing worms who squeal with glee,
Pink and yellow whirl and twirl,
Every droplet makes them swirl.

A daisy dons a water crown,
While violets try not to frown,
The breeze joins in, a playful guest,
Teasing blooms, they spark and jest.

Each splash a quirky ballet,
Nature's stage in humorous play,
Grass tickles their feet in glee,
As critters join the jubilee.

Bright fragments light the dampened day,
While giggles drift and trail away,
A dance of colors, free and bold,
In this whimsical world, behold!

The Scent of Memory and Moisture

Nostalgic scents fill the air,
While droplets swirl like a fair,
Fragrant whispers of the past,
In puddles, chuckles seem to last.

Captured laughs in the cool rain,
Every splash tells tales of fun pain,
Sniff the air, what do you find?
A tickling breeze both sweet and kind.

Wobbly woodies stomp around,
As joy's perfume hugs the ground,
Hummingbirds in a crazy flap,
Join the giggle in a rapid lap.

Each aroma leads to delight,
As flowers sway, what a sight,
Memories dance in the damp affair,
Laughing together, beyond compare.

A Symphony of Blossoms and Showers

In the orchestra of the downpour,
Lilac notes tumble, birds encore,
Seasons play their gentle tune,
While rain dances 'neath the moon.

Bright petals flutter in a chase,
As droplets drum a floral race,
All the blossoms hum a cheer,
In this concert, laughter's near.

The wind strums on the willow trees,
While daisies sway, they've caught the breeze,
Comedic chords of color bloom,
Nature's giggles fill the room.

So let's embrace this raindrop rhyme,
With flowers bouncing, it's fun time,
A symphony, sweet and spry,
While blossoms skip beneath the sky.

Fluttering Hearts in a Tempest

When love's a dance, oh what a sight,
It twirls and swirls, takes off in flight.
In stormy gusts, it howls with glee,
Chasing after cakes, wild and free.

A soggy shoe, a squishy heart,
Hopscotch in puddles, a classic art.
With thunder's laugh and lightning's cheer,
We skip like children, no room for fear.

A soggy greeting, a drippy kiss,
Slapstick love in a watery bliss.
Chocolate umbrellas, they float away,
Love's silly circus in nature's ballet.

So, sway, oh love, with cheeky flair,
In tempestuous fun, we haven't a care.
For hearts that flutter, indeed can glide,
In the rain's embrace, we'll silly-bide.

Hues of Harmony and Hail

Colors burst forth, a riotous show,
With hailstones tap dancing, oh what a blow!
Drenched in laughter, joy rides the breeze,
Daffodils giggle as they bend their knees.

A monsoon of giggles, skies full of glee,
We spin like tops, wild yet carefree.
Come join the chorus of nature's refrain,
Where giggling flowers sing in the rain.

Where daisies frown and tulips pout,
We laugh at the gloom, making fun about.
With rainbows peeking, we cheer and sing,
A palette of joy, let the laughter ring.

Through the drizzle, our spirits soar,
Collecting chuckles from every door.
In hues of harmony, we'll always remain,
With smiles painted bright, merry and unchained.

Lightly Falling from Heaven

Drops descend like playful sprites,
Tickling roofs in silly sights.
They bounce on noses, with playful flaps,
Creating a symphony of giggly claps.

Clouds parade in fluffy gowns,
While puddles wear capes of shiny crowns.
We jump in rain boots, splash as we go,
Like clowns in a circus, stealing the show.

An umbrella topsy-turvy whirls,
In the wind's embrace, it twirls and swirls.
Laughter erupts with each sudden gale,
As we gallop through puddles, leaving a trail.

Softly falling, oh what a ball!
Each droplet's a chuckle, we hear them call.
In a dance with the sky, we're giddy and light,
With joyfully soaky, a splish-splash delight!

The Language of Drenched Petals

A chatter of colors, they giggle and grin,
With tongues of rain, the drenched fun begins!
Each flower whispers secrets of cheer,
In puddles of mirth, we draw near.

A waltz on the sidewalk, slippery and slick,
While raindrops tickle, we do a quick flick.
Sopping wet socks, it's a fashion craze,
We strut and we stroll through nature's maze.

In squishy delight, we revel and play,
With mud pies tossed, in a frolicsome way.
The language of blooms speaks laughter anew,
In this quirky town, where mischief just grew.

So join in the jive, feel the splash and dash,
In the choir of raindrops, we giggle and clash.
With each drenched petal, let smiles take flight,
In our comical garden, everything's bright!

Liquid Light on Blossom's Edge

Droplets dance like tiny clowns,
Making flowers wear silly crowns.
Sipping sunshine, giggling loud,
Nature's joy brings a jolly crowd.

Mirthful raindrops jiggle and sway,
Tickling petals in a playful way.
Every bloom in a swirling spin,
Laughing together, let the fun begin!

The Veil of Soft Petals

A curtain of color drapes the ground,
Soft whispers of laughter are all around.
Each flower's blush tells a funny tale,
As they wiggle and laugh, they never fail.

With dainty sways, they dance in the breeze,
Tickled by raindrops, they wobble with ease.
A giggle erupts from a shy little bud,
As clouds chuckle over the midst of the flood.

Transient Beauty Under Grey Skies

Clouds wear frowns like grumpy old men,
While blossoms chuckle, they'll bloom again.
Joking with raindrops that slip and slide,
They've got humor and petals full of pride.

Silly shapes twist in puddles so round,
Reflections of laughter bouncing all around.
The drizzle sings loud like a wet tambourine,
Making every flower a part of the scene.

Shattered Rainbows on Garden Floors

Colors collide and burst into cheer,
Splashes of hue, nothing to fear.
Giggles from lilies and chuckles from bees,
A riot of mirth rides the soft summer breeze.

While clouds sing a tune in playful dismay,
Tiny blooms wiggle, come out to play.
With each little droplet a joke to be found,
The garden is happier when splashed all around!

The Music of Blooms Beneath the Clouds

Flowers dance in showered glee,
Laughing at the bumblebee.
Raindrops play a merry tune,
As petals giggle 'neath the moon.

Each drop a note, a playful splash,
With yellow blooms in quirk and dash.
'Twirling violets take the lead,
While tulips try to plant a seed!

Gentle Reflections in the Garden's Soul.

Sunshine peeks through fluffy gray,
Wet leaves chuckle, gutter-sway.
The daisies tell a soggy joke,
While umbrellas sigh and soak.

Chasing snails on slippery trails,
With muddy boots and fancy fails.
Laughter spills like raindrops round,
As nature's giggles swirl the ground.

Whispers of Fallen Blooms

Once upon a time, they stood,
Now they tumble, oh so good!
In puddles deep, their secrets hide,
As squirrels play and jump and glide.

A chatty rose, with droopy head,
Complains to daisies, 'I'm misled!'
But violets wink, with cheeky cheer,
'Come join the fun, the show is near!'

Dance of the Drifting Fragrance

Swaying scents upon the breeze,
Tickle noses, bring us ease.
In raindrops, flowers spin and twirl,
As ladybugs begin to whirl.

The scent of laughter fills the day,
As tulips waddle, come what may.
With every splash, a giggle bursts,
And nature's joy is what we thirst!

Serenity in a Fragile Touch

Tiny twirls in captured air,
Dancing fairies unaware.
On the street, they spin and glide,
Throwing giggles far and wide.

Droplets fall and cause a splash,
Whispers of a joyous crash.
Soggy shoes and laughter loud,
Nature's folly, quite a crowd.

Bright umbrellas turn to slides,
As folks find their awkward rides.
With a slip and merry cheer,
The wettest day is really here!

So let them float, those funny hats,
Rainy jokes and crazy chats.
In this dance of misty glee,
Life's a chuckle, can't you see?

The Art of Falling Flowers

Beneath the clouds, they take their dive,
Frequently miss the ground alive.
Landing, somewhat, with much grace,
They create quite the silly place.

With each gust, a silly swirl,
Decorates the noses of every girl.
Oh, the fun of dodging drops,
Giggles occur when slippery flops!

Cupped in hands, a fleeting green,
Nature laughs—oh, what a scene!
Wishing on a dampened whim,
Who knew flowers would so swim?

When puddles form, what a delight,
Splashy battles waged in light!
To track those petals on the run,
Chasing blooms is so much fun!

Drenched in Silent Poetry

Splat! A drop whirls past the ear,
While flowers giggle, oh so near.
With each splash, a secret told,
A silly dance, bright and bold.

Windswept whispers fill the air,
As laughter clashes without a care.
Follow the puddles with some flair,
Watch out now—there's joy to share!

Muddy paths, a squishy sound,
With every step, the joy is found.
Splashing colors all around,
In this chaos, bliss is crowned.

Hold your breath, here comes the phase,
Silly hops in a watery maze.
What's more fun than slipping free?
Nature mocks, it's comedy!

Awakening the Hueman

In drizzles, laughter's what we find,
Nature's jokes, a silly kind.
Swirling hats flop on the head,
As blooms waddle where we tread.

Each thread of rain, a playful spark,
Unruly fun from dawn till dark.
Flip-flops flying, chasing round,
As muddy sides announce the sound.

Bouncing kids with mischief bright,
Singing rhymes, taking flight.
Drenched in giggles, don't refrain,
Life's a riot in the rain!

With every splash, a spark ignite,
Awake the soul with pure delight.
Let's embrace this quirky stream,
A funny life in nature's dream!

Whirls of Life in Flurries

Little twirls, a dandy spin,
Watch them dance, let the fun begin!
Through puddles they go, splash and sway,
Quirky laughs in this delightful play.

A bunny hops, a squirrel grins wide,
Jumping joys, they cannot hide!
A splash of color, a wiggle, a flop,
In this merry whirl, we never stop.

Oops, a slip on sudden mud!
Giggles echo with a thud!
Nature's pranks bring mirth anew,
In jolly chaos, we are a crew.

So twirl about and greet the day,
With leaps of joy, come join the fray!
Life's a jest, and here we reign,
As we race through gold and rain!

Serene Soliloquy of Softness

A whispering breeze, oh so light,
Teasing leaves with sheer delight.
Clouds giggle, while skies sway,
In this soft hush, we skip and play.

A fluffy cat on a window ledge,
Dreamy paws, a cozy hedge.
It yawns, then leaps in lazy arcs,
Creating giggles, the day embarks.

Beneath the tree, a picnic spread,
Sandwiches fly, 'til they're all smeared.
Food fights bloom, no one gets mad,
In this soft mess, all hearts are glad!

So let us wriggle in quiet glee,
For life's a soft song, as you can see.
With every heard, silly note, we glide,
In this sweet softness, we reside.

Cascades of Nature's Cloak

Cloaks of green, a laughter spree,
Raindrops twinkling like jubilee.
A squirrel slides down a leafy tube,
Oh, what fun in this leafy cube!

Cheeky frogs leap with a bounce,
What a sight, let's all announce!
Their splashes make merry tunes,
Underneath the chuckling moons.

A duck waddles by with a quack,
In muddy races, there's no lack.
With slippery antics, it glides along,
Turns the day into a silly song.

When skies drip laughs, and breezes sing,
Every leaf joins in, to cling.
Nature's cloak giggles, dances proud,
In cascades of joy, we gather 'round!

Blessings from the Water's Caress

A splash of joy, a giggling stream,
Turns the world into a dream.
Here comes the splash with a boisterous cheer,
Tidal waves of laughter, oh dear!

Bright-eyed frogs aim for the show,
They jump and croak, putting on a glow.
In puddles big, they twirl and dive,
With bouncy leaps, they feel alive!

A soggy dog bounds with a bark,
Slipping, sliding, a comedic arc.
It shimmies and shakes in every tone,
Wettish wins, it takes the throne!

So let the waters play their role,
In every drop, laughter takes hold.
With each splash, we make a mess,
In this watery dance, we are blessed!

Melancholy Blooms in Soft Showers

When blooms get drenched, they look confused,
Like they just found out they've been misused.
With droopy heads, they start to sway,
Wondering why they can't just play.

A rose complained, 'I hate this vibe!'
A daisy said, 'I'd rather hide!'
While lilacs groaned in moody tones,
"Someone please call our garden gnomes!"

But then a daffodil burst forth with cheer,
"Look! We're getting a refreshing beer!"
The raindrops laughed; they made a toast,
To tired flowers, who cheered the most.

So now they dance in silly loops,
Forming muddy, happy flower troops.
They twirl and spin, not caring a bit,
In a soggy, giggling flower skit.

The Secret Life of Drenched Sprigs

When clouds decide to shed a tear,
The greens all jump, it's time for cheer!
Forget the sun and all its rays,
Time for splashes and slippery plays!

Young sprouts, they slip on puddle floors,
While daisies tell their rainy chores.
"Who knew that soggy could feel so neat?
I think I'll start my own wet dance beat!"

Old tulips laugh, their worries shed,
"Look at us, like paintbrushes spread!"
They splat and splurge, like kids at play,
In a game of splash, they'll win the day!

So in this world of water's joy,
Each sprig a giggling little boy.
They wear their drenched attire with pride,
In soaking wet, they do abide.

A Ballet of Droplets and Petals

A raindrop pranced upon a bud,
'This stage is set; let's make some mud!'
We'll twirl and spin with all our might,
Dancing under clouds, oh what a sight!

The lilies laughed, "We'll take the lead,
With moves so fancy, we'll surely succeed!
Watch out, we're gliding, swooping low,
Like ballerinas in a flower show!"

But then a smear from a pigeon flew,
It landed smack on a flower too.
The cast just gasped, then broke in giggles,
"A little splat adds to our wiggles!"

With sprightly joy, the stage was set,
Each bloom forgot their little fret.
Through drizzles and drops, they find their grace,
In this grand ballet, they share their space.

Cherished Moments in Mist

With dawn's soft haze and dew so bright,
The flowers snicker, "What a sight!"
"Is this our spa day, or am I drenched?
I think I need a towel, I'm pinched!"

A dainty rose pranced with a grin,
"Let's make a splash, we're sure to win!'
With pollen rain and a polka dot,
They dance through mists in a joyful plot.

Forget their worries, the weather's fine,
In every droplet, a chance to shine.
Each flower giggles, as breezes lap,
Reveling 'neath this funny mishap.

So here's to moments drenched in fun,
With joyful sprigs, we'll never run.
In mists of laughter, we shall play,
Thankful for this soggy ballet!

The Softness Between Storms

Flowers wear hats made of dew,
They dance like crazy, it's true.
Wind tickles their little tips,
Laughing as each raindrop drips.

Clouds giggle, shrugging with glee,
A soft waltz on a slippery spree.
The garden throws a grand parade,
In mud, they gleefully wade.

Bumblebees buzz with a cheer,
Wobbling, they balance on a sphere.
Colors clash in a humorous quest,
Each bloom vying to look its best.

As puddles form, they jump and splash,
Creating a messy, joyful crash.
In nature's jest, they spin and sway,
Turning gray skies to a colorful ballet.

Legacy of the Blossom's Embrace

In the garden's playful mess,
Blooms giggle in a soft caress.
Each flower tells a joke in mime,
As they bloom in carefree rhyme.

Raindrops bounce, a merry dance,
They trip and slip, what a chance!
Petals get stuck in muddy shoes,
While sunbeams throw confetti hues.

Bees with sunglasses buzz around,
Wearing tiny hats, making sound.
Each blossom tosses back a grin,
While sipping nectar from within.

The wind blows a cake of air,
Sending giggles everywhere.
Nature laughs in every hue,
Creating joy that's always new.

When Colors Meet the Sky

Colors collide, a bizarre sight,
As blooms debate who's the most bright.
They argue like children at play,
In nature's wonderful, wild ballet.

The raindrops join with a splish-splash,
Painting the world in a whimsical clash.
Yellow and pink do a funky twirl,
While purple does flips, giving a whirl.

Clouds giggle with a fluffy cheer,
Sharing secrets that only they hear.
In the chorus of laughter, they bend,
As each color tries to outtrend.

With every drop, the colors ignite,
Creating a canvas of sheer delight.
In the sky's embrace, they wildly play,
A funny festival in nature's display.

Heartbeats Beneath the Soft Shower

Under the sky with drops of fun,
Flowers bounce like popcorn on the run.
Each one giggles, making a mess,
Dressed in raindrops, in joyous dress.

The breeze throws a party, light and airy,
Spinning blooms, oh how merry!
A chorus of laughs from the leafy crowd,
As raindrops tumble, so proud, so loud.

Snails slide in their comical race,
On slimy trails, oh what a chase!
Dancing in rhythm, losing all fears,
Nature's laughter flows like cheers.

Beneath the timid, whispering rain,
Every heartbeat shares the refrain.
With pitter-patter stories to tell,
Life stitches together, laughter to swell.

When Blooms Meet the Sky's Tears

When flowers dance with drops so bold,
They giggle softly, tales of old.
They sway and spin like little clowns,
As puddles form in silly crowns.

With every splash, they chuckle loud,
A comedy show beneath the cloud.
Their colors run, a wild display,
Creating art in a playful way.

Bees wear tiny raincoats tight,
Dodging raindrops, a comical sight.
While butterflies twirl, wings dripping cheer,
In this wet circus, they have no fear.

So let the sky weep, let it pour,
The garden laughs, we just want more.
With every drop, a joke unfolds,
In nature's theater, laughter molds.

Eclipsed Colors in a Deluge

Colors swirl in a watery mess,
Splat in the puddles, chaos, no less.
Tulips wear streaks of watery hue,
While daisies giggle, 'What can we do?'

Raindrops play tag on the petals' tip,
Wet flowers wiggle, giving a slip.
With each hiccup and wobble so slight,
They bloom their laughter under moonlight.

A robin slips, on a rainbow's trail,
Bouncing back with a quizzical wail.
Their giggles echo through the sweet air,
In this riot of hues, worry's laid bare.

So paint me a picture, all mishmash and fun,
Where colors collide, and laughter is spun.
In this garden, joy's the decree,
For every droplet holds hilarity!

Nature's Chorus of Glistening Hearts

Oh listen closely, the flowers sing,
In the rain, they wear bling-bling.
With droplets glistening on leaves and bloom,
They harmonize bright in nature's room.

Laughter bursts from the tangled vines,
As worms waltz under the water signs.
The sunpeeking shyly, a timid guest,
Can't help but laugh at their wet jest.

Clouds tumble down, a comedy spill,
Pansies play hide, with marigolds' thrill.
The wind, a jester, whirls them around,
In this giggle fest, joy knows no bound.

So let the raindrops play their tune,
In the garden's laughter, we'll find our moon.
For every heart tinged with drop-shaped spark,
Roots deep in humor, dancing in the dark.

Melodies of the Weathered Garden

In a garden where giggles float,
The daffodils sing in a silly coat.
With each raindrop, a new joke is spun,
They hop right up, 'Oh this is fun!'

Old trees shake their branches with glee,
While squirrels tumble, 'Look at me!'
With a clap of thunder, they dance in place,
A lively show in this wet embrace.

Colors collide, a chaotic sight,
Sunsets and storms, a comedic fight.
Gardens adore this playful spree,
While raindrops boogie like they're free!

So laughter echoes through every vine,
In the weathered garden, all things align.
With jests and jives, in laughter, we'll soar,
For rain only brings us to crave more!

Drizzle's Serenade on Pollen

Drops dance on flowers so bright,
Jigs by the bees, what a sight!
Hats made of leaves, all in a row,
Twirl away giggles, that's how we flow.

Mushrooms prance like silly clowns,
As raindrops play on puddle crowns.
A bug with a hat, oh what a tease,
Sips from a cup that's filled with breeze!

Chasing the wind, they slip and slide,
Nature's laughter we can't abide.
In puddles they splash, what a delightful mess,
Joyful as flowers in their Sunday dress!

A harvest of giggles, a rain-soaked day,
Even the worms wobble and sway!
With little umbrellas made out of fronds,
They march in a band, to our joyous songs!

Petal-Laced Memories

Wobbly blooms in a weathered vase,
They dance to the tunes of a slip-up grace.
A bumblebee tripped, fell on a face,
Laughter erupts, oh what a place!

Flower hats drifting in the breeze,
Chasing the clouds with playful ease.
A rogue sunflower takes a spin,
Tickling toes where giggles begin!

Crickets serenade alongside pies,
With whipped cream clouds in the clear blue skies.
Soggy socks from a joyful stomp,
A dance off with daisies, it's quite the romp!

Even the raindrops take time to play,
Racing down leaves in a wild ballet.
Nature's mischief, a comedic affair,
Memories sprout, floating in the air.

A Tapestry of Watered Hues

Colors are laughing in vibrant swirls,
A canvas alive with giggling curls.
Squishy slippers on wiggly grass,
Nature's palette — no need for class!

Daffodils twirl in their Sunday best,
While raindrops gather for a laugh-fest.
Dancing puddles reflect cheeky grins,
As garden gnomes take out their violins!

The chubby frogs cheer, "Come join the fun!"
Under the drizzles, they leap and run.
With a plop and a splash, they steal the show,
Jokes from a squirrel as they steal a tow!

With socks mismatched in rain-soaked glee,
The world is a sketch, come paint it with me!
Laughs in the garden, a whimsical roam,
In nature's embrace, we find our home!

Blooming in a Silver Mist

Morning arrives with giggles galore,
Silver dew drops, they bounce on the floor.
Blossoms are chuckling, tickled by air,
As rolling clouds form a fluffy chair.

Butterflies plotting a premature flight,
Whispering secrets of day turning bright.
A daisy sneezes, oh bless you my dear!
Sprinkling laughter like confetti, oh dear!

Giggling winds stir the lavender fields,
Where whispers of humor, nature yields.
The tulips are plotting a joke or two,
"Why did the daffodil cross the dew?"

With silver mist cloaked in bright bouquet,
Every flower joins in the fun of the day.
So tiptoe through gardens, let laughter be free,
In blooms that are grinning, it's all jubilee!

The Tincture of Wet Wonders

A flower danced in a puddle,
With splashes that made quite a muddle.
It swirled, it twirled, oh what a sight,
Petal pals laughing with pure delight.

A bee slipped in, buzzed like a fool,
With wings all wet, it slipped from its school.
A wiggly worm joined the fun parade,
While nearby raindrops laughed and played.

The sunshine peeked, all warm and bright,
Making puddles shimmer, oh what a light!
Yet every splash sent giggles around,
In this garden, joy is unbound.

The flowers sing, in colors bold,
With jokes about rain, never old.
Every droplet makes a pun so grand,
In this lovely, silly wonderland.

Mosaic of Liquid Grace

Look at the daisies, all drippy and bright,
They're wearing their necklaces made of pure white.
They jiggle and giggle as raindrops fall,
A slippery slapstick, they're having a ball!

A ladybug slid on the slick, shiny ground,
Turning to tumble, it spun round and round.
With its red spots gleaming, it launched one last try,
And went straight up into the soft, cloudy sky.

The grass is now slick, it's a slide, oh so sweet,
Where giggling ants take a wild little seat.
They zoom past each other with splashes and squeaks,
These chubby little critters are playing for weeks!

So let's raise a toast to downpours that tease,
To flowers that giggle and dance with the breeze.
In this humor-filled patch, there's much to embrace,
As we wade through a world that's a mosaic of grace.

Droplets that Sing to Blossoms

Oh, listen close, the flowers croon,
To the rhythm of raindrops that make them swoon.
Each drip and drop has a tune to share,
Creating a concert in the fragrant air.

The rhododendron with its wide-open face,
Spills out a chuckle like it's in a race.
While tulips tease with their silly sway,
In this wet wonderland, it's a cabaret!

A frog with a crown leaps in for a dance,
Mopping up puddles, he takes a chance.
While fireflies giggle and switch on their lights,
As petals and raindrops set off their delights.

So join in the laughter, grab a front row seat,
As blossoms serenade with each little beat.
The droplets compose a wild symphony,
In this puddle of joy, we're all fancy and free!

The Unearthed Symphony of Gentle Rain

Beneath the clouds, a quirky show,
As flowers strike a pose with a ducky toe.
The wind plays flutes, the droplets beat drums,
While bumblebees buzz to their own funky sums.

The curtains of soft rain began to rise,
As daisies and lilies rolled their eyes.
They wink at each other, it's quite the affair,
With a splashy encore in the cool, humid air.

The giggling tulips whisper their dreams,
While raindrops pirouette with sparkling beams.
An audience of worms gives their best applause,
To this nature-made show that leaves us in awe.

So here's to the fun that rain likes to bring,
With flowers that dance, sing, and hop into spring.
In this symphony, all laughter, no pain,
Life's a quirky melody, thanks to the rain!

Whispers of Blossom and Drop

In the garden, flowers sigh,
When clouds roll in, the blooms get shy.
They huddle close, what a silly scene,
As droplets fall, they giggle and preen.

A daisy slips, falls with a plop,
An astoundingly awkward flop!
The roses roll their eyes, so bold,
Saying, "Watch out! Here comes the cold!"

The tulips twirl, oh what a show,
Dancing lightly, side to tow.
But with a drop, they stumble and squeak,
Their whole arrangement made quite unique!

So the garden bursts with laughter bright,
As nature dons her rainy delight.
Each bloom a character, wild and whacky,
Beneath the clouds, feeling quite tacky!

Tears of the Flora

Oh look! The blossoms weep and cry,
With drippy drops from the cloudy sky.
A sunflower frowns, says, "Oh dear me!"
While lilies ponder, "Is it just tea?"

The brook's now full, oh what a splash,
The violets trip and make a dash.
"Watch out for puddles!" they squeal and shout,
But their slippery dance ends with a pout.

The pansies giggle, quick on their feet,
Jumping over streams, what a treat!
But just when you think they have it made,
An unexpected slip, oh what a parade!

In this wet world, they find a way,
To laugh and prance, come what may.
Even when tears from above fall down,
These blooms wear smiles, never a frown!

Dance of the Dew-kissed Blooms

In morning's light, the flowers sway,
Covered in droplets, bright as day.
A daffodil twirls, says, "Look at me!"
While the marigolds giggle, wild and free.

The hydrangeas start a conga line,
Bumping and grinding, feeling just fine.
But with a slip, they sway and spin,
Who knew the rain could make them grin?

The geraniums chuckle, do a jig,
While tulips wiggle, feeling so big.
"Can we dance faster?" one petal sighed,
And they all agreed, then slipped and slid.

So in the garden, fun they seek,
With every splash, they squeal and squeak.
A riot of colors, laughter, and cheer,
All in the dance, nothing to fear!

Gentle Cascade of Color

A gentle fall, a vibrant shower,
Bright colors drip from every flower.
A peony spun with each plop and thud,
Said, "Do you think this is good for mud?"

Carnations splash with each lovely drop,
They yell, "A pool party! We can't stop!"
Hydration's key, come jump right in,
But sandals and soil? Where to begin?

Orchids prance in puddles galore,
With antics to spare, they reach for the floor.
"Look at us float!" they cheerfully boast,
Until banana peels bring out a ghost.

And so they play, this merry troupe,
With laughter and splashes, they form a loop.
In this wild garden, antics abound,
Where every drop is a joy unbound!

Petal Kisses in a Storm

In the garden, laughter swirls,
Droplets dance like giggling pearls.
A snail slides down, a slip and slide,
Waving to bees, with a bumpy ride.

Umbrella blooms, bright and bold,
Twirling under clouds, a sight to behold.
A chorus of raindrops taps on my hat,
While bugs join in, a slippery chat.

Chasing worms that wiggle and weave,
Each splash a knock on nature's eaves.
Soggy socks, oh what a joke,
I trip on leaves, and then I poke.

Yet through the riot, joy holds sway,
In squishy shoes, we laugh and play.
Each drop's a giggle, a sparkly tease,
Oh, what a whirlwind, oh, what a breeze!

Garden's Eulogy in Drizzle

A daisy droops, its head held low,
Mourning the sun, oh where did it go?
With each drop, it sighs and leans,
A flowered funeral for sunny scenes.

Puddles form, little lakes of cheer,
Soggy shoes and clumsy veers.
A dandelion in a tuxedo sprout,
As we slip and slide, there's laughter all about.

The roses giggle, their colors like blush,
They couldn't care less in the rainy hush.
A deluge of snickers, a rib-tickling fate,
As worms throw a party, isn't it great?

With each soft splash, the tales unfurl,
Life's a comedy in a wet swirl.
In this drizzle, the laughter won't cease,
A garden's eulogy turns into a feast!

Evaporating Radiance

The sun peeks out, a shy hello,
While puddles sparkle, putting on a show.
Clouds get confused, they gathered and spaced,
Balloons in the sky, all flying with grace.

Giggles rise with the steam in the air,
And frogs in tuxedos leap without a care.
The dance of the drops, each a tiny sprite,
As the sun takes a bow, it's quite the sight.

Blades of grass wear raindrop crowns,
While daisies wink in their soggy gowns.
A parade of worms strut down the lane,
As rainbows emerge, we giggle again.

With every laugh, the air turns bright,
A stage of whimsy, pure delight.
A vaporous waltz of colors we see,
Oh, evaporate all woes, let's just be!

Rainy Reveries of Silken Touch

A tap on the window, a gentle tease,
Raindrops dance like whispers in trees.
Twirling squirrels in their cozy coats,
Join the parade with tiny toads' quotes.

Sunshine spills, but in drops it hides,
As kittens chase raindrops, with playful slides.
Wet fur and laughter fill the day,
Every splash leads to a new cliché.

Blossoms giggle, a soft, silly sound,
As puddles reflect all the joy around.
Watercolors swirl, a playful twist,
In this joyous mishap, nothing's amiss.

Breezy chuckles in a playful fray,
Each droplet's a jest as they dance and sway.
In the rain, we find our youthful clutch,
Embracing the rush of a silken touch!

A Symphony of Scented Drops

On a sunny day I peek,
Caught a whiff, oh what a freak!
Raindrops dance amidst the blooms,
A floral party, watch it zoom!

Ladybugs in tiny hats,
Inviting ants, with silly chats.
They twirl and spin without a care,
While pansies giggle everywhere!

Bees buzz in a buzzing choir,
Fleeting scents that take you higher.
In this wet and whimsical spree,
Nature's quirks make glee for free!

Join the flash mob, make some noise,
With fragrant flowers, all the joys.
Let's splash around, no time to rue,
Oh, what fun with scents anew!

Gentle Embrace of Dew

Morning whispers soft and sweet,
Tickling toes, where earth and greet.
The grass is wet, a squishy tease,
With droplets clinging to the trees.

Slippers sliding, oh what a sight!
A clumsy dog gives everyone fright.
He shakes it off, with a goofy bark,
As kids run wild, igniting spark!

Dewdrops trickle down my nose,
Laughing at the funny woes.
Look at me, a frosty mess,
Nature's joy in its own dress!

As the sun peeks, the show won't stop,
A splash of giggles with every drop.
In this embrace, we dance and play,
A silly joy to greet the day!

Echoes of Floral Grace

A trumpet flower with a flair,
Hoots and howls fill the air.
Roses rolling in a race,
Bumbling bees in a windy chase.

Sunflowers swaying in a row,
Humming jokes, putting on a show.
They nod their heads, a silly crew,
With laughter bright, and laughter true!

Each petal spins with laughter loud,
A goofy dance, we're nature's crowd.
Daisies whisper, come and play,
We're fun and frolic every day!

So join the party, don't be late,
Giggling blooms just can't wait.
In this field of humorous grace,
We celebrate with a bright embrace!

Blossoms Caressed by Clouds

Up above, the sky takes charge,
Fluffy clouds that loom so large.
They tickle blooms with every breeze,
Whispering secrets, oh, what tease!

A thunderstorm with jokes galore,
Knocking on doors, "We want more!"
Each droplet falls, a splashy cheer,
Come play with us, the flowers leer!

Pansies giggle, violets grin,
Waltzing on the breezy spin.
While raindrops tumble, oh what fun,
As blossoms sing, their day begun!

So let the clouds just play their game,
With every drop, we join the fame.
In laughter's rain, we find our way,
Celebrating blooms in disarray!

Fleeting Dreams on Moistened Streets

A squirrel slipped on a shiny leaf,
It danced a jig, quite beyond belief.
Puddles laughing, splashing round,
As I chased after, slipped to the ground.

Umbrellas turned like upside-down hats,
Cheers to the raindrops, our little spats.
Rubber ducks race on a gleaming tide,
My wet socks whisper, 'Oh, what a ride!'

Giggling umbrellas take off unnoticed,
As the clouds in the sky seem to be the boldest.
While laughter mingles with the splashing spree,
We waltz through puddles, happy and free.

The streetlights flicker like a broken joke,
As I dodged a splash from an unkind stroke.
Chasing shadows 'neath the dreary gray,
Who knew the downpour would save the day!

Rain's Embrace of Tender Blossoms

With every drop, a bloom gets a drink,
Each sip like coffee, causing it to blink.
Daisies giggle, swaying in the breeze,
While wildflowers ponder life's little tease.

A snail slides by in a jacket of dew,
Laughter echoing, who knows where it flew?
The tulips say, 'We'll sway all day!'
As rhymes of joy leap from the bouquet.

Petunias yell, 'Bring on the storm!',
They wave their petals, all cheery and warm.
A frog croaks jokes in a soft muddy tone,
Turns every splash into a heartwarming phone.

Buds in puddles spin dreams of delight,
Making rain dance like a comic delight.
With their laughter shared, the moment expands,
In this quirky world, we join hand in hand!

Falling Lights and Floral Echoes

Luminous drops fall like giggles from high,
Roses snicker, saying, 'Oh my, oh my!'
Petals prance in the wet, wild storm,
While daisies plot their dance and perform.

A wind chime laughs, tickling the air,
Funny little echoes, as if unaware.
They bounce and twirl, in a rhythm divine,
Creating a melody, sweet and benign.

Caterpillars twirl in a raindrop ballet,
While the clouds overhead decide to play.
With colors so bright, they trip through the sky,
Where even the sun beams a buoyant sigh.

Fragrant splashes land with a light-hearted grace,
Each droplet turning every frown to embrace.
As flowers chatter and blossoms take flight,
In this funny dance, the world feels just right!

Echoes of Lush and Liquid

Oh, how the puddles reflect our glee,
As green things grin and sway with a spree.
The daisies tumble like clowns in a show,
With their vibrant colors putting on a glow.

Mirrors of joy on the slippery ground,
Hopping in puddles, laughter unbound.
Grass takes a sip, and the daisies crest,
In a wet world, we find our zest.

While raindrops play tag with the daisies bright,
The world becomes silly in this soft light.
Funny faces drawn on each raindrop's fall,
As nature giggles, let's join in the call!

Each splash a story, each spin a song,
In the embrace of the storm, we belong.
So grab your coat and let's dance for a while,
In this echo of laughter, let's leave with a smile!

Nature's Silk in a Sudden Shower

Tiny dancers twirl so sleek,
As raindrops make their cheeky peek.
They slip and slide on leaf and stem,
Oh what a sight, a funny gem!

Umbrellas bloom like flowers bright,
While squirrels dash, a comical fright.
They shake their tails, a laugh ensues,
In nature's game, they cannot lose!

Splish, splash, all around they go,
Chasing drops in a wiggly show.
Birds join in, with a flappy cheer,
Who knew a drizzle could bring such cheer?

So let the droplets gleefully fall,
Nature's giggle, the best of all.
When skies cut loose in playful streams,
It's all a jest, or so it seems!

Echoes of Fragility in the Wind

Whispers float on gusty breeze,
Like tumbling laughs from swaying trees.
A leaf takes flight in a comic swoop,
While worms below just spin and loop.

A blade of grass, it bends in prayer,
As insects join the windy affair.
They dance in circles, not a care,
While nearby blooms wear a floral flare.

A raindrop lands on a flower's face,
It giggles loud, then runs, in haste!
The petals blush, how rude, they say,
At nature's jokes, they grumble and sway.

But in this madcap swirling gust,
Their worries fade, they laugh; they must.
Among the jesters with soft spins,
Life's fragile echoes turn to wins!

The Colors That Weep

When clouds hang low, the colors cry,
They giggle drops, as wash goes by.
A rainbow sneezes, bright and bold,
A humorous sight to behold!

Yellow stains the blue, it's true,
As orange chuckles, getting the cue.
Violet sighs, in a glittery show,
As laughter swells and colors flow.

The hues parade, with splats and swirls,
In nature's palette, giggles twirl.
Who knew hues could play so nice?
In puddles deep, they dance on ice!

When harmony's struck in zestful hue,
Nature's canvas becomes anew.
So join the laughter, splash around,
With colors that weep, joy is found!

Garden Serenade Under Clouds

In the garden, under gray,
Flowers feign a grand ballet.
Dance with daisies, leap with glee,
To the rhythm of drizzly spree.

Bumblebees buzz in a striped tux,
While worms below are stuck in 'ux.'
They wiggle low, with joyful sighs,
Creating laughs in muddy highs.

A cabbage winks, with leaves in curls,
As raindrops drip and swirl in whirls.
The daisies giggle, "What a day!"
While clouds above join in the play.

So here's to gardens, drenched in fun,
Where nature's antics have just begun!
In showers soft, there's joy to find,
In this serenade, laugh and unwind!

Solace in a Floral Shower

Dancing blooms upon the ground,
As raindrops play a joyful sound.
Slippery shoes begin to spin,
Who knew gardening could cause such din?

A bee with goggles, buzzing loud,
Wants to join this clumsy crowd.
Pick up the flowers, don't they know?
They're in a splash zone, put on a show!

Bright colors mix like a smoothie treat,
Funny how mud feels like a sweet sheet.
Slide in circles, a floral delight,
Who knew chaos could feel so right?

Laughter echoes, nature's own game,
Just a day, but never the same.
In a garden where mishaps grow,
We dance and spin, oh what a show!

Ephemeral Wishes in the Wetness

Wishing wells turned upside down,
With drizzles wearing a flowery crown.
Each drop's a wish, slippery and fleet,
Even the daisies can't keep their feet!

A chubby snail with a tiny grin,
Waves to the puddles with a spin.
Bouncing, splashing—who would have thought?
A wet circus of giggles should be caught!

Everyone's hair is a frizzy surprise,
Questions about style meet cloudy skies.
So let's embrace the squishy parade,
With umbrellas turned boats—how are we swayed?

Watercolors drip from the clouds,
Giggles echo, they're that loud!
Wishes fly as droplets dance,
In this whimsical, rainy romance!

Hues of Love in a Gentle Flood

When colors run like silly dreams,
A rainbow bursts at the seams.
The puddles smile, like art in play,
Dancing hearts in a splashy ballet!

Here come the ducks, all in a row,
Quacking loudly, they steal the show.
With feathers wet, they're quite the sight,
And join in laughter, oh what a flight!

Nature's paintbrush goes wild and free,
Creating mismatched glee in the spree.
Splattered colors, a giggling mess,
Love in hues, we couldn't care less!

With each drop that hits the ground,
A new joke blooms, laughter unbound.
In this colorful storm, side by side,
Who knew love could be this wide?

When the World is a Liquid Palette

A canvas drips from water's sway,
Throw on your raincoat, come out and play!
Brushstrokes of joy, with splashes of cheer,
Creating a giggle that's perfectly clear!

Frogs jumping in, the splash brigade,
With each leap, it's a rainbow parade.
Why walk when you can make a big splash?
Life's a canvas—it's a colorful bash!

Umbrellas turn into floating boats,
As dreams drift by like playful goats.
Silly dances under the gray,
Turn the gloom into sunny ballet!

With swirls of color everywhere found,
The laughter echoes, a joyful sound.
In this puddly world, we'll twirl and glide,
Painting life's story with laughter and pride!

www.ingramcontent.com/pod-product-compliance
Lightning Source LLC
Chambersburg PA
CBHW071127130526
44590CB00056B/2838